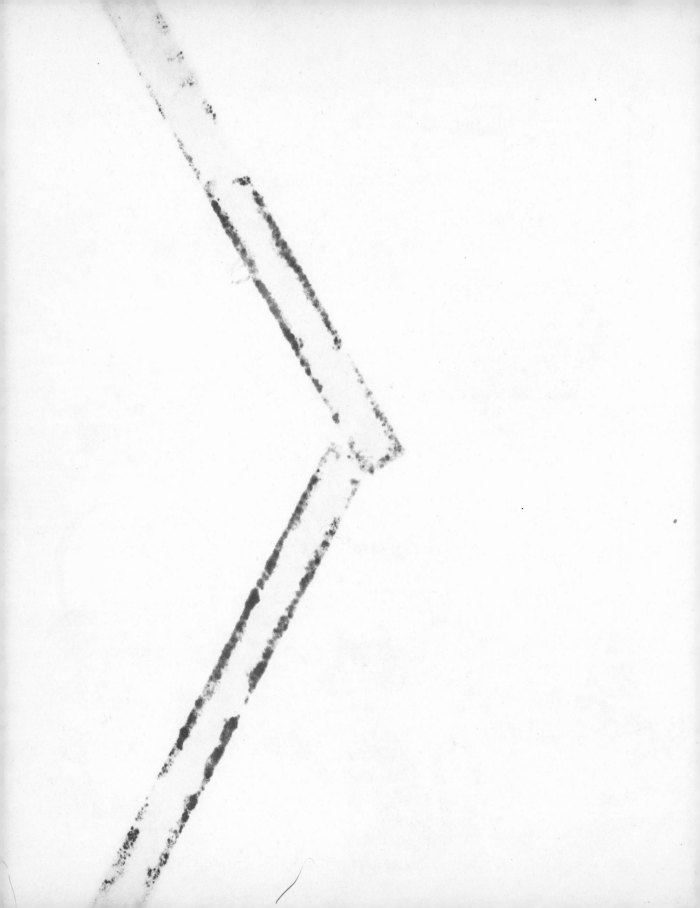

A HOLIDAY BOOK
Jewish Holidays

BY BETTY MORROW
AND LOUIS HARTMAN

ILLUSTRATED BY NATHAN GOLDSTEIN

GARRARD PUBLISHING COMPANY
CHAMPAIGN, ILLINOIS

Especially for Art and Ruth

Holiday books are edited under
the educational supervision of

Charles E. Johnson, Ed.D.
Professor of Education
University of Georgia

For reading the manuscript and checking the accuracy
of its content, the authors and publisher are grateful to

Dr. Bert S. Gerard
Temple Administrator and Director of Education
Westchester Reform Temple, Scarsdale, New York

Contents

1

Five Thousand Years of Holidays

It is sundown. The house is full of the smells of good food. On the table the lighted candles gleam. The room is gay with laughter and singing. The children are getting ready to play games. This is the beginning of a Jewish holiday.

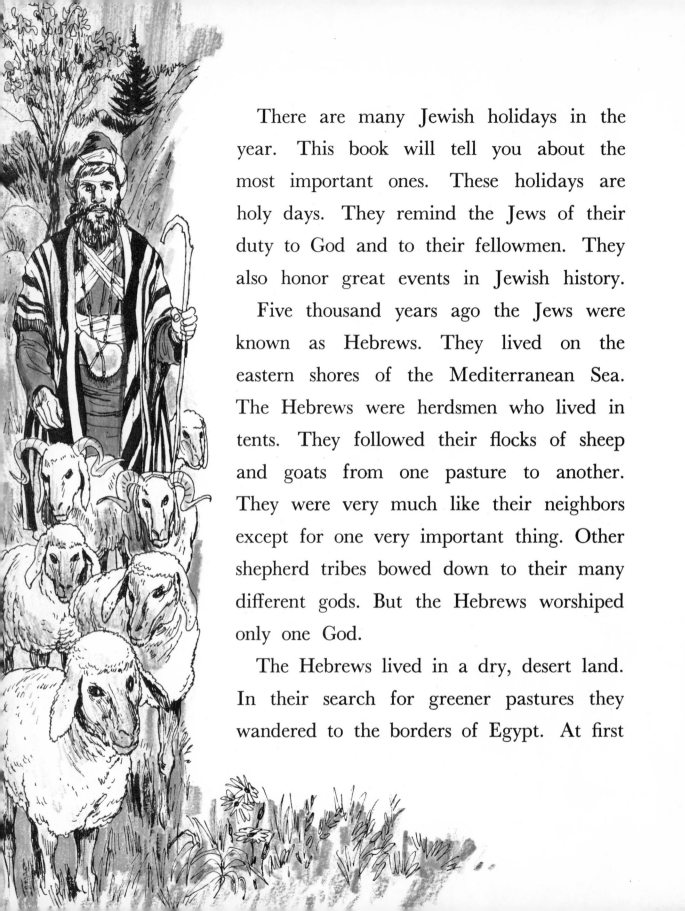

There are many Jewish holidays in the year. This book will tell you about the most important ones. These holidays are holy days. They remind the Jews of their duty to God and to their fellowmen. They also honor great events in Jewish history.

Five thousand years ago the Jews were known as Hebrews. They lived on the eastern shores of the Mediterranean Sea. The Hebrews were herdsmen who lived in tents. They followed their flocks of sheep and goats from one pasture to another. They were very much like their neighbors except for one very important thing. Other shepherd tribes bowed down to their many different gods. But the Hebrews worshiped only one God.

The Hebrews lived in a dry, desert land. In their search for greener pastures they wandered to the borders of Egypt. At first the Egyptians left them alone. Then the pharaoh, or king, grew afraid of strangers. He made the Hebrews his slaves and forced them to build the great cities and pyramids of Egypt. For many hundreds of years the Hebrews were cruelly treated.

Then Moses became the leader of the Hebrews. He led them out of Egypt. They wandered in the desert for forty years. The Jews believe that this was God's way of preparing them for freedom. During this long march something happened that the Jews have never forgotten. The Bible tells the story.

Moses went to the top of a mountain called Sinai. When he returned, he said that he had talked with Jehovah. Jehovah, or God, had then given him the Ten Commandments. These simple laws told the Jews how they should act toward God and each other.

Moses said that he had made an agreement with God. God promised to watch over the Hebrews and protect them. The Hebrews in return promised to obey God's laws forever. This agreement is called The Covenant.

At last the Hebrews entered a land called Canaan. They defeated the tribes who lived there and took the country for

their own. The Hebrews became farmers as well as herdsmen. In Egypt they had learned to build cities and temples. Now they built a great Temple for the worship of God in their capital city, Jerusalem.

Time passed. The Hebrews began to quarrel among themselves. They split into two kingdoms, Israel and Judah. The word Jew comes from the word Judah. Finally, the people of both kingdoms became known as Jews.

Their neighbors, the warlike Babylonians, wanted the Jews' land. Time and time again their large armies attacked the two kingdoms. The Babylonians destroyed the temple in Jerusalem and took a large number of Jews to Babylon as captives. Many others fled to Egypt. After many years the Jews in Babylon were allowed to leave. They returned to Jerusalem and

10

rebuilt the Temple. Later on the Romans
conquered them and destroyed the Temple
a second time. By now the Jews were
living in many different countries around
the Mediterranean Sea.

Wherever they lived, the Jews continued
to worship one God. This was not an easy
thing to do. In many pagan lands the
rulers were thought to be gods. They were
afraid of the Jewish idea of one Supreme
Being. Often these rulers would kill the
Jews because they could not force them

11

to accept the religion of their conquerors.

After the coming of Christianity the Jews were still cruelly treated. Sometimes they were forced to live in special parts of the cities called ghettos. Jews were not allowed to hold certain jobs or to go to regular schools. Sometimes they had to leave their homes. Even in the twentieth century, Adolf Hilter, dictator of Nazi Germany, destroyed more than half of the Jews of Europe.

But Jews never stopped worshiping God in their own way. They never stopped observing their holidays either. From earliest times Jewish holidays have been celebrated in both the synagogue and at home. They begin most often with prayer and a family feast.

The holidays begin in the evening. They last from one sundown to the next. The Jews have their own religious calendar. It measures the months by the moon. These moon months are not the same length as our legal months. That is why the Jewish holidays do not fall on exactly the same date each year.

In the United States today there are three large religious groups among Jews–Orthodox, Conservative, and Reform. Orthodox Jews try to follow very closely the way in which Jewish holidays have always been observed. Conservative Jews have tried to blend together the older ways of celebrating with new ideas. Reform Jews have shortened the holidays, dropped many old customs, and introduced new ones.

13

2

The Sabbath, Holiday of Free Men

Most holidays come only once a year. The Sabbath is celebrated every week. It is the day set aside to rest and to honor God. The Fourth Commandment says: "Six days shalt thou labor and do all thy work, but the seventh is the Sabbath of the Lord thy God."

The Sabbath begins at sundown Friday and lasts until sundown on Saturday. In many Jewish homes no work of any kind is allowed after the Sabbath begins. Food for the Saturday meals is prepared before sundown on Friday.

There is a special holiday bread. These twisted loaves are called *hallah*. The Bible says God sent manna from heaven to feed the Jews when they wandered in the desert. The manna, or food, was found on the ground. On Friday they gathered manna for two days, as no work was done on the Sabbath. That is why there are often two loaves of hallah on the Sabbath table.

After school on Friday the children polish the candlesticks and the wine cup. They help their mother spread a white tablecloth and set out their finest dishes. Then the children put on their best clothes and wait

for their father to come home. If he is an Orthodox or Conservative Jew, he may visit the synagogue first.

The father often brings home flowers for the Sabbath table. As he enters the house he says, *"Shabbat Shalom"* (a peaceful Sabbath). He places his hands on his children's heads and blesses them.

At sundown mother lights the Sabbath candles and says a blessing, "Blessed art Thou, O God, King of the Universe, who has made us holy with Thy commandments, and commanded us to kindle the lights of the Sabbath." Some families light a candle for each child. The candles are a sign of the peace and light that the Sabbath brings.

The father lifts the wine cup and says a prayer. The wine is a sign of God's gift of the fruits of the earth to all men. Everyone takes a sip of wine. Then a blessing is said over the hallah, and the Sabbath meal begins.

When the meal is over, some families sing Sabbath songs, while other families will attend Friday evening services at the synagogue or temple.

A favorite hymn welcomes the Sabbath this way:

The sun on the treetops no longer is seen.
Come, gather to welcome the Sabbath, our Queen.
The Sabbath is coming, the holy, the blest.
And with her good angels of peace and of rest.

Again on Saturday morning too there are services at the synagogue. The rest of the day is free for *Oneg Shabbat*–the delight of the Sabbath. For some families this will mean quiet games and visiting; for others more active fun. For all it is a day of remembering God and a day of rest. It is truly a "Queen" of days.

At the end of the Sabbath there is a

18

ceremony called *Havdalah.* The word means "parting." This ceremony always takes place in the synagogue, and sometimes at home. Here the ceremony begins when the children can see three stars in the evening sky. They light a special candle made of many colors. The father opens a box of spices. The sweet smell reminds the family of the happiness of the day that is ending.

The family sings a last hymn together.

A good week, a week of peace,
May gladness reign and joy increase.

The father holds his hands before the candle. He explains that the light of the flame is the Sabbath. The shadows on the wall are the ordinary days of the week. Everyone says, "A good week to you," and the candle is put out.

The Jews are not the only people who observe a day of rest. Christianity keeps Sunday as a day of special worship and of rest. The Mohammedan day of rest is Friday. But the Jews were the first people to set aside a day of the week for everyone to rest from his labors.

This is why the Sabbath is sometimes called the "Holiday of Free Men."

20

3

Rosh Hashanah,
The New Year

Rosh Hashanah is the Jewish New Year. Like everyone else, the Jews celebrate the beginning of the calendar year on January first. But their religious year begins on the first day of Tishri. This is the seventh Jewish month and comes in September or during October.

Fall was a very important season for the ancient Hebrews. In their part of the world little rain fell. During the summer the land became drier and drier. The rains came during the fall months or not at all. If there was a drought, the crops would be poor during the coming year. Many people would starve to death.

The Hebrews believed that the drought came because they had broken God's laws. In this way the New Year became a day of judgment. Jews today believe that on Rosh Hashanah God judges each person for his actions during the past year. That is why the Jewish New Year is a serious holiday, as well as a happy one.

At sundown, after prayers, the family gathers for the New Year's meal. They welcome the new year by wearing new clothes. The hallah on Rosh Hashanah is sometimes shaped like a ladder. It is shaped this way to show that people can go up or down in the world. In the year to come the choice depends on them. The father gives the children a slice of apple dipped in honey. This is a sign that the new year will be full of good things.

The following day there is a service in the synagogue. The children look forward to the blowing of the *shofar*. This is the

hollow horn of a ram, a male sheep. The tip is cut off, and the horn is blown like a bugle. The shofar called the Jews together when Moses brought them the news of the Ten Commandments. Today it reminds them of their agreement to obey God's laws. The shofar makes a wild and stirring sound.

The blowing of horns at the New Year is a very old custom all over the world. In ancient times people made a loud noise to frighten away evil spirits. They felt that the spirits were very close and powerful on New Year's Day. Jews adopted this custom, not to ward off evil spirits, but to recall great events in their history.

At New Year's time the Jews, like many other people, resolve to lead better lives. Worshipers used to go from the synagogue to a stream of water. They would shake crumbs from their pockets into the flowing stream. This meant they were casting off their sins.

Legend says that God opens the Book of Life on Rosh Hashanah. This records everyone's deeds and thoughts during the past year. God reads the book and decides everyone's fate for the new year. Those who have been good will have a year of happiness. Those who have been bad will have a year of unhappiness. And at Rosh Hashanah Jews send greeting cards with the wish, "May a good year be recorded for you."

The ten days starting with Rosh Hashanah are known as the "Days of Repentance." People who are truly sorry for their mistakes can ask God's forgiveness. Then their names may still be written in the Book of Life for a happy year.

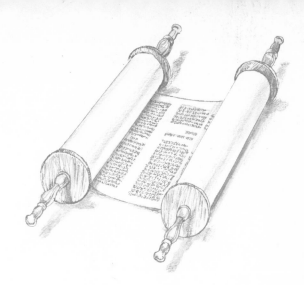

4

Yom Kippur, The Day of Atonement

During the Days of Repentance people used to visit everyone they had wronged during the past year. Even if they had only thought an evil thing, they were expected to ask forgiveness.

This was an exciting time for the children. The house was always full of people. Everyone who came was given a piece of honey cake. The cake stood for the sweetness of the Torah. This is the name given to the first five books of the Bible. They tell the story of the early days of the Jews. By following God's law as laid down in the Torah, people would be happy in the year to come.

Yom Kippur, or the Day of Atonement, comes at the end of the ten Days of Repentance. The Bible tells how the ancient Hebrews sent a special goat out into the wilderness each year. They believed that

the goat would take all their sins away with him. This cleansing from sin was called *kippur* in Hebrew, and the day, or *yom*, came to be known as Yom Kippur.

People think that our word "scapegoat" comes from this ancient custom. We think of a scapegoat as someone who suffers for the sins of others.

Jews no longer believe that a goat can take away their sins. Instead they ask God to forgive them.

On the Sabbath before Yom Kippur, the hallah is baked in the shape of a circle. This is a sign that man hopes to return to God and become "at one" with him.

On Yom Kippur itself everyone goes without food for twenty-four hours. Only the very young and the very sick are excused. Fasting on Yom Kippur is not considered by the Jews to be a punishment.

It is a way of showing that a person has the strength to live a good life in the year to come.

The synagogue has a special look on Yom Kippur. The Ark, the holy chest that holds the scrolls of the Torah, is covered with a white cloth. This is the color of a newly washed lamb. It is the color of purity. The rabbi wears white robes, and there are often white flowers on the altar.

Yom Kippur is the day for honoring the good deeds of those who have died. The living promise to do good deeds of their own in the year to come.

The evening service begins with the chanting of the *Kol Nidre*, or All Vows hymn. The haunting melody touches the souls of the worshipers, just as the shofar stirred their hearts on Rosh Hashanah. It is chanted as the sun goes down.

Now the most solemn moment of the Jewish year is at hand. Each person must ask God to forgive him and all others for the sins they have committed. Everyone in the world is included in the Yom Kippur prayer: "May all Thy children unite in one fellowship to do Thy will with a perfect heart."

From early morning until sundown on the following day a service is held in the synagogue. The service ends with one long blast of the shofar. The gates of judgment are closed. The record of a person's life now stands in God's book for another year.

5
Sukkot,
A Double Thanksgiving

Sukkot is the Jewish harvest festival. It comes during October, five days after Yom Kippur. Sukkot has many names. One of them is the Feast of the In-gathering.

Farmers in ancient times lived in villages. Each day they went to work in their fields outside the villages. At harvest time there was a great deal to do before the rains came. There was no time to travel back and forth from village to field. So farm families built huts of branches in the fields. The children wove wild flowers into leafy roofs. Father tied the first sheaf of grain to the doorpost. Mother hung the biggest bunch of grapes from the roof. At night the family could look up through the branches and see the stars shining in the autumn sky.

At last the harvest was gathered. The grapes were pressed into wine or dried for raisins. The storehouses were full of wheat and barley. The sight of so much food made the people want to sing and dance with joy. There was feasting for several days. The people made offerings of bread and wine on the village altar. There was a big celebration at the great temple in Jerusalem.

Later, most of the Jews in Europe lived in cities. They were no longer farmers, but they still celebrated the harvest festival. They built huts or booths, called *sukkahs,* as the farmers had. Sukkot is sometimes called the "Festival of Booths." It also reminds the Jews of the booths lived in by their ancestors in the desert.

Usually, the fence or the back of the house served as one wall of the booth.

During the eight days of Sukkot the family ate their meals there. Sometimes the rain came through the leafy roof. Then everyone grabbed the dishes and ran for the house. Even that added to the fun.

Today in the United States, few people have sukkahs at home. Instead, everyone helps to build a large sukkah in the courtyard of the synagogue. Then the children decorate their sukkah with harvest fruits, vegetables, and flowers.

There are also special services in the synagogue. The rabbi and some of the people hold palm branches in one hand and a yellow citron in the other. They wave them to the north, south, east, and west to show their thanks to God for His harvest gifts.

The citron is called *ethrog* in Hebrew. It is a fruit like a lemon. It has a pleasant

smell. When the Jews lived in the ghetto, many of them were very poor. Citrons were expensive. So six families would buy one together. By the time Sukkot was over, the citron was bruised and battered. But each family had enjoyed its fragrance.

Sukkot is not only a time of thanksgiving for the good things of the earth. It is also the holiday when the Jews thank God for the Torah. This thanksgiving takes place on the last day of Sukkot. It is called *Simhat Torah,* or "Rejoicing in the Law."

The sacred scrolls of the Torah are taken from the Ark and carried around the synagogue. Everyone joins in the parade.

Boys and girls carry flags. On the top of the flagstaffs are candles in hollowed-out apples. After the parade the children are given nuts and candies.

There are many other harvest festivals all over the world. One of the most famous is the American Thanksgiving. The Pilgrims were great Bible readers and knew about the festival of Sukkot. Perhaps they thought of it when they planned their first Thanksgiving in the new land.

6

Hanukkah,
The Feast of Lights

In December, Jewish homes are filled with songs and laughter and the flickering lights of candles. This is Hanukkah, the Feast of Lights. Hanukkah celebrates a great victory of the Jewish people.

Two thousand years ago, Jews were ruled by a cruel Syrian king called Antiochus.

He drove the Jews from the Temple in Jerusalem and ordered them to worship the Greek gods. Without mercy Antiochus murdered those who refused. The Jews fought back strongly. They were led by a father and his five brave sons called the Maccabees.

They led a band of warriors into hidden caves high in the mountains. Time after time the Maccabees swooped down from the hills. Each time they put the Syrian soldiers to flight. More and more Jews joined the Maccabees. At last the Jewish army was strong enough to take Jerusalem back from the Syrians.

They found the Temple filled with altars to the Greek gods. Weeds grew in the courtyards. The Jews set to work to clean the Temple. When it was ready for the worship of God, they paraded through the streets. They sang and carried torches as they marched. Then a great service of rejoicing was held in the Temple.

This is the true story of Hanukkah. There is also a beautiful legend about it which has been told for hundreds of years.

When all was ready for the service, no one could find any of the special oil for the Temple's holy lamp. At last one tiny jar was discovered. It held just enough oil to burn for a single night. But the lamp over the Ark was supposed to burn night and day.

Then came the miracle. The lamp burned for eight days until new oil was ready. This miracle is remembered every year at Hanukkah. Each family brings out a special candlestick called a *menorah*. It has eight branches, one for each day of the miracle.

At dusk on the first night of Hanukkah, the family lights the first candle. They say a special prayer. On the second night two candles are lighted. Three are lighted on the third night, and so on until all eight candles are burning. Each night an extra candle is used to light the others. This is the *shammash,* or "helper."

The children sing:

O Hanukkah, O Hanukkah, come light the menorah.
Let's have a party, we'll all dance the hora.
Gather round the table, we'll give you a treat.
Dreydls to play with, *latkes* to eat.

Latkes are potato pancakes, a special Hanukkah food. The dreydl is a little square top. On the four sides are Hebrew letters standing for the words *Nes Gadol Hayah Sham* meaning a great miracle happened there. A player spins the dreydl

and sees which letter comes up on top.
Sometimes he must put candies or nuts
into the center of the table. If he is
lucky, he may take some out.

Some people think the dreydl game was
invented during the time of the Maccabees.
Antiochus would not let the Jews gather
to study the Torah. So they thought of a
way to protect themselves. While they

45

were reading, the students kept a top on the table. If soldiers came, they could pretend they were just playing a game.

Today it is the custom to give children presents on each night of Hanukkah. In some homes the finest gift is saved until the last night. The children also receive money called Hanukkah *gelt*. Sometimes this is a bag of chocolates that are wrapped in shiny gold paper to look like coins.

At Hanukkah, darkness comes early. The holiday is usually close to December 21, the shortest day of the year. After that the days grow longer, and spring is on the way.

From earliest times, many different peoples have celebrated this important period. The early Greeks danced on the hillsides with lighted torches. Later the Romans held the feast of Saturnalia with lights and dancing. The Christmas lights of modern times are an echo of those long-ago festivals. So are the lights of Hanukkah.

The Jews gave this ancient celebration a new meaning. The word Hanukkah means "dedication." The Jews remember how the temple was dedicated in the days of the Maccabees. The Hanukkah candles honor the men and women who gave their lives for the right to worship in their own way.

7

Purim,
A Springtime Carnival

Purim is the gayest of the Jewish holidays. It is a time for parties, plays, and dances. Purim comes on the fourteenth day of the month of Adar. That usually falls in March.

Purim started in days when Jews were living in Persia. It honors Queen Esther whose story is in the Bible.

Esther was a beautiful young Jewish woman. She was married to Ahasuerus, the great Persian king. Her cousin Mordecai was the leader of the Jews in Persia.

The king's prime minister was a proud and wicked man named Haman. He was furious when Mordecai would not bow down before him. And Haman had always hated the Jews. Now he told the king that the Jews lived by their own laws, not by Persian laws. He tricked Ahasuerus into giving him permission to kill the Jews.

When Esther heard of Haman's plot, she hurried to the king. She told him how Haman had tricked him. Ahasuerus was touched by her courage. He ordered the prime minister hanged on the gallows he had built for Mordecai. On the day the Jews were to be killed, they rose up and destroyed Haman's army.

Purim celebrates this victory of the Jews. On Purim, children put on fancy costumes. They act out this story of Esther and Ahasuerus.

The story of Esther is read in the synagogue. Whenever the name of Haman is mentioned, the children try to drown it out. They stamp their feet and wave noise-makers over their heads. And they are also

drowning out the memory of other men throughout history who have tried to destroy the Jews.

Purim is a time of gift giving. Friends exchange gifts of food. Presents and gifts or money are collected for the poor.

In olden days children put on masks and went from house to house singing:

Today is Purim, tomorrow no more.
Give us a penny and show us the door.

People gave the children special cakes called *hamantaschen*. They are still served today. These three-cornered cakes are filled with sweetened prunes or poppy seeds. They are supposed to look like Haman's hat. Actually, they are shaped like hats worn by the police in the ghettos of the Middle Ages.

Most people who study history think that the story of Esther is only a legend. The end of winter, however, has always been a time for rejoicing. In many lands people put on costumes and parade through the streets, dancing and singing.

The ancient Persians greeted spring with such a carnival. Two bands of soldiers pretended to have a battle. Some carried the banners of darkness. Others carried the flags of the sun. The soldiers of light and springtime always won.

The Jews enjoyed the carnival when they were in Persia. Historians believe they took the idea of the battle and wove the story of Esther around it. Instead of light battling darkness, the Jews conquer Haman.

8

Passover, A Festival of Freedom

Passover is the most famous of the Jewish holidays. *Pesach,* as it is called in Hebrew, is really two holidays in one. It comes in March or April and is a joyous welcome to spring. For years shepherds celebrated at that time. They sacrificed a lamb and prayed that their flocks would multiply and grow strong.

Later on, the festival took on a new meaning. It celebrated the escape of the Hebrews from Egypt.

The days before Passover are a busy time. The houses are given a special cleaning. Everything sparkles and shines. Extra boards are put into the table to make room for guests. It is a tradition that no one shall be turned away from the Passover feast. Some homes have a special set of dishes used only for Passover.

A feast is a part of most Jewish holidays, but on Passover it is especially important. The ceremony that includes the feast is called a *seder*. This is the Hebrew word for "order." During the seder the story of the escape from Egypt is told and special foods are eaten in a special order.

The table does not look as though it is set for a feast. In the center are three

pieces of dry, cracker-like bread, called *matzoh*. A lamb bone and a roasted egg are side-by-side on a platter. There are parsley and bitter herbs. A special bowl is filled with salt water, and another bowl holds *haroseth*. This is a good mixture of chopped nuts, apples, and wine. And it is colored brown with cinnamon.

After the candles are lighted and the blessing is said, the youngest child asks this

56

question: "Why is this night different from all other nights?" The father explains: "Once we were slaves in the land of Egypt and the Lord our God brought us out of there with a mighty hand and an outstretched arm."

The child asks questions about the seder food. The father tells him that the matzoh is like the bread the Jews ate when they left Egypt. The parsley, a sign of spring

and new life, is dipped into salt water before it is eaten. This is a reminder of the tears of slavery. The bitter herbs have the taste of slavery. The cinnamon-colored haroseth is the color of the clay the Hebrews used in making bricks for the pharaoh. The lamb bone recalls the days when the Jews were shepherds.

Through the centuries, many songs, poems, and stories have been written about Passover and the escape of the Jews from Egypt. These have been set down in a book called the *Haggadah*. The stories are read by the father, or by other members of the family, in answer to the child's questions.

Early in the seder the father breaks one of the matzohs in half and hides it under a pillow. It is his duty to guard the matzoh. If the children can find it, he has to give them a reward to get it back. The

seder cannot end until everyone has had a bit of the hidden matzoh.

After the first part of the Haggadah has been read, delicious foods are served. Roast chicken, stuffed fish, and sponge cake are seder favorites.

Wine is an important part of all Jewish feasts. At Passover there is an extra glass that no one touches. This is for the prophet Elijah. It is said that some day he will

come down from heaven with great news—all men everywhere are to be free forever. The most exciting moment in the seder comes after dinner when the door is opened and Elijah is invited to enter.

The little children cannot wait until it is time to sing the special Passover songs. One favorite is a tongue-twister about a little goat, called "A Kid for Two Farthings."

This is the last verse:

Then came the Holy One, praised be He,
And smote the Angel of Death,
That slew the butcher that slaughtered the ox,
That drank the water that quenched the fire,
That burnt the stick that beat the dog,
That bit the cat that ate the kid,
That father bought for just two bits:
One kid, an only kid.

The story of Passover is in the Bible too, in the book of Exodus. The Hebrews wanted to leave Egypt, but the pharaoh refused to let them go. The Bible says God decided He would punish the Egyptians. Each family's eldest son would die. The Hebrews were told to sacrifice lambs, as was customary in the spring, and to mark the doors of their houses with the lambs' blood. Then the Angel of Death would "pass over" their homes and spare them.

Even the pharaoh's son died. The pharaoh was heartbroken. He told the Hebrews they could leave Egypt at last. They ate a hurried meal before they left and packed food. There was no time to bake regular bread, as the dough has to rise. Instead they took some unleavened dough with them and baked flat bread, or matzoh, in the desert.

After the Hebrews had gone, the pharaoh changed his mind. He sent his soldiers to stop them. The Egyptian chariots caught up with the Hebrews at the Red Sea's edge. According to the Bible, the waters parted and the Hebrews were able to cross over on dry land. Then the waters rushed back and drowned the Egyptians. The Hebrews were free!

The spirit of freedom is important not only to Passover, but to all Jewish holidays. Freedom is also important to all Americans.

The words of Moses appear on the great Liberty Bell in Philadelphia. "Proclaim liberty throughout the land to all the inhabitants thereof."

The spirit of the Jewish holidays will live on until "all men, everywhere shall be free forever."

PRINTED IN U.S.A.

GAYLORD